Clarity

A Collection of Poems

Centra Smith

Clarity: A Collection of Poems
Queening, LLC
Detroit, MI USA

Edited by: Sylvia Williams
Cover Design: Centra Smith

© Copyright 2017 Centra Smith
ISBN-13: 978-0-692-86217-9

All rights reserved.
No part of this publication may be reproduced, stored in a retrieval system, or transmitted in any form or by any means, electronic, mechanical, photocopying, recording or otherwise, without the prior written permission of the publisher. Key Term definitions are from the website, Dictionary.com. All Scripture quotations are from the *Holy Bible*, King James Version.

For speaking engagements and other information about permission to reproduce entries from this book, please contact:

Centra Smith
www. Queening.art
Queening.llc@gmail.com

Clarity

[klar-i-tee]

noun

clearness or lucidity as to perception or understanding; freedom from indistinctness or ambiguity.

Dedication

I dedicate this book to you. To the one who really doesn't quite understand or "get" what "this life" is all about. To the one who has often questioned the fuzziness of life and just what it means. I've been where you are and truthfully, sometimes I still find it a bit fuzzy. But now, my trust and my sight is on someone Greater, who holds the keys to all that I am and all that I'll ever will be. So to you, whoever you are, I love you and I pray that my experience through words will help you see life just a little bit clearer. There is more for you…so…much…more.

Introduction

The purpose of this collection of free verse poetry, or the *spoken word* is to capture real life personal issues for the troubled, broken, hopeless, uninspired, and lost, in hopes of bringing about a liberation and restoration. Growing up in the city of Detroit and being raised by a single mother of two, certain values and methods of thinking, such as self-perception, confidence, my voice, and a clear understanding about the real world were not instilled or ingrained in me until I had furthered my education and reached adulthood. I suffered for many years in my mind, not knowing my value, identity, or purpose. So, I allowed myself to be negatively influenced and pulled away by the many voices and thoughts of people in my then surrounding environments. It wasn't until the summer of 2012 when I was rejected from my college's nursing program that I decided to sit out of college for two years. I needed to regroup. Only then did I begin to awaken and discover a new *self,* my *true voice,* as well as a sense of *purpose* influenced richly by my Christian faith. It was during those same years that I learned the power of words, and I wrote a collection of poems and short stories, and started and finished my first completed draft of my soon-to-be published memoir.

The conception and birthing of *Clarity* was a direct result of my own personal journey, which encompassed sexual abuse, peer pressure, promiscuity and discovery, while in pursuit of understanding my true value, identity and purpose in the world. As I began to evolve and mature, so did my awareness and my voice through poetry. My perspectives began to change, in that I began to see a disconnect—a broken relationship—between a fallen world and a patient, passionate, unconditional-loving, and forgiving God.

My objective when writing poetry is to keep it simple. Although the subjects that I speak on are serious, real, and complex, I have found and still believe that using simple, colorful language will make a stronger and lasting impact on my audience. I pray this book reaches you and brings healing and clear insight into what, or to *Whom,* you are searching.

Author's Note

This book consists of a collection of title-less poetry and is open to personal, unique interpretation. However, specific words, phrases, and even sentences are bolded or italicized for the sole purpose of illuminating both importance, subject, and intent of each poem.

A **story** can't be told unless it has been written.
Unspoken words can't impact lives
but lay hollowing lifeless on the inside.
I don't know where I'm going with this,
but I noticed how time slows down
when you start *paying attention.*
Time slows down
when you start
paying attention.

For so many years,
she wanted to be,
that
girl.
You know?
That
girl.
That girl that got all the attention
and was hated by women.
She wanted the look
of perfection,
but instead
what she received
was
perpetual
rejection.
So she switched roles a lot,
whatever seemed suitable
at
the
time.
Conformity was a normality
but on the inside
she was stricken deep.
Filled with pain…
Filled with frivolity.
No, she wasn't alive
but she was dying.

And the tears
... of her soul
could not stop crying.
She had grown into someone that
she did not recognize.
Masked
by
deceptions.
Disguised
by
a
bunch of lies.
Drawing closer.
Knocking
on
the door
of her inevitable demise.
She was consumed
in confusion.
Her thoughts,
more specifically
her
identity,
was a fusion of
cultural
hype
and human-bred malpractices.
And boy was she

losing
bad.
Worldly advertisements fed
her
unhealthy
habits
and like a bandit,
she stole away every superficial piece,
every seemingly clothe to layer,
to cover up an
ever present void
that was
always
there.
But she didn't care,
because she was destroyed
by the pride
of her
eyes
and the lust
of her
flesh.
Not knowing that she was falling
head-long
down
deep
into a ditch.
Or better yet, mud,

as she continually wallowed around in
the vomit of her mess.
She
kept
digressing
...and digressing.
Falling
like light speed.

Down
to her
knees.
LOST.

My mother once told *me*
when I was a little girl,
probably around the age two
or three,
how I loved to look out
the living room window
just to see what I could see.
I never quite understood
what was before me.
But I'm guessing now,
just looking back,
the **curiosity** of my mind
was what drove me.
It imploded my sense of
awareness
not knowing all the while
that **His eyes were watching me**…

My mother once told *me*
when I was a little girl,
probably around the age two
or three,
how I loved to look out
the living room window
just to see what I could see.
I never quite understood
what was before me.
But I'm guessing now,
just looking back
the **curiosity** of my mind
was what drove me.
It imploded my sense of
awareness
not knowing all the while
that **His eyes were watching me**

When I look in the mirror,
who do I see?
I see a reflection that is distant and unfamiliar to me.
"Who is she?"
This face that is staring back at me.
The face of a woman,
a girl,
I thought I once knew.
But the cares of this life have estranged her
and the pain that she feels so intensely
has maimed her.
So she begins to cry...
and then she stares hard in the mirror,
frustrated with anger,
she screams to the Lord,
"Why?!
Why didn't you just let me die!"
Instead of me enduring this sorrow,
hopelessness,
and pain inside.
"Why must I survive?"
I feel trapped in a body
That plays with my mind
It has a will of its own
and I have absolutely no control over it
so I feel so alone.
I see no beauty.
I see no grace.

I see no life.
All I see is this earthen face
of a woman,
a girl,
I thought I once knew.
But the more I look,
The more I'm confused.
I feel so used.
I feel so empty.
I've completely lost my **identity**.
"Who is she?"

I remember when things weren't so complex,
when things weren't so... complicated.
If I could only go back to the days
when I would play,
to that 6-year-old little girl again
who would spin and spin,
and would imagine so freely of
flying in the wind.
She was full of dreams
and full of laughter
and her mind wasn't cognizant
of the hereafter.
She was consumed in her moments,
not worrying about time.
Wasn't thinking about boy-crushes
or even heartbreaks.
It wasn't even a concern of her mind.
She was completely oblivious
to the demands and darkness of life.
Lucid.
If I could only go back to those days...

if I could only tell her...

I would walk up to her slowly

and gently whisper into her ear

saying,

"Love-child take your time,

play like no one is watching

and have

"No Fear."

I **was** the curses sown deep.
Seeds of my enemy
implanted into my identity,
my DNA structure.
And so I ruptured.
Burst.
Into all kinds of tainted lust.
Like a wildfire
chased by the wind
that driven me into the arms of captivity
who I naively,
yes, so easily
trusted
to no end.
I was tattooed in sin.
Looking for love in all the wrong places,
I was faceless.
Masked
by the inventions
of lies.
A shadow of misery.
A pathetic disguise
of materialistic stuff
that was dear to me,
but it wasn't enough.
No...
It wasn't enough.

And it couldn't cover up
my void.
Or the fact that my own
father ravaged and destroyed
my innocence,
which was a death sentence
to the life
that I only hoped to live.
A dream deferred.
A childhood ridden
because of one wrong adult decision.
And what was left of me was...
the dozens of cracked bottles
that brimmed over
with the many tears,
intensified fears,
and so many lost years
of unheard cries
from a little girl's
early...
demise.

He told me
that I was beautiful.
Just last night,
girl he looked at me
with loved filled eyes
beneath the twilight sky
and we kissed
so passionately.
Girl I was completely…
 swept …
off…
my feet.

He told me that I was beautiful
and I in turn
believed him
time after time,
after time again.
He used words like
"girl you are so beautiful"
that unlocked
the gates of my very soul,
my heart.
And so I allowed him
to enter.

To come in
into my secret place.
As I delved
deeper
into his rich black
warm skin.
Taking hold of his
oh sweet face,

he in return wrapped his big

arms so tightly
around my small framed body
and at that moment,
everything
became totally…
non-existent.

I just knew this emotion
could never end.
It was like a potion
where I butterflied in
the deep blue ocean of
his trance.
As the words
"girl you are so beautiful"
danced all around me.

We lost consciousness.
I was so caught up
in his beautiful love song.
I was so caught up
not knowing that I
was falling headlong.
Deeper.
And deeper.

But his lips…
got ever so sweeter
whispering into my ear
of all the wonderful things
that I desired to hear.

Girl he was patient.

Chile he was so kind.
He was everything
that I could ever dream
or pray for,
and girl
did I mention
that he was fine?!
But I knew…
I knew…
that he wasn't mine.

I was given a premonition of
this very moment,
but I didn't want
to own it.
And so I turned a blind eye to
what God had already spoken.

I ignored all the signs.
I ignored all the warnings.
I ignored what was plain to see
because I was too curious
and girl I was too…
horny.

I was lured by his bait.
He was careful and calculative
of all the steps that it would
take
for me to be
received by him.
Characterized by tact
and just like that

the light of his love

quickly but surely
faded to black.

He told me that I was beautiful.
That he loved,
would never leave,
and even promised
to marry
me.

He told me…
Yea, girl, he told me…
He told me lies!
He was Satan in disguise,
and this I know
when he never
said
goodbye.

Leaving me broken,
ashamed,
and opened
wondering…
"Why?"
Asking myself over
and over and over again,
*"Why did I not listen to you
Lord?*
*"Lord why did I ever waste
my time?"*

Lust will leave you blind.
So be careful...
with who you allow
to hold the keys to your most
precious possession.
Your heart.

Lest you find yourself
naked, scrambling around in
the dark, when what you
perceived as love began to
unravel. Shatter. Humiliate.
Expose. Shame. Abuse.
Fall apart and CHECK OUT on
you.

Beautiful are the eyes of him
who sees you
for who you really are
in Him.
Virtuous.
Who discovers
and recognizes a pearl,

an exquisite jewel
of great price,

when he sees one.
Knowing that his claim of
you
can only be gained by the
permission
of thee One,
who loves you the most.

So be careful Eve...
understand that you are a
gift
wrapped beautifully.
So precious, that neither time
nor wear or tear
could depreciate you.
But instead
His **Love** increases your value.

So be careful...
And wait for Him.
Wait on God.
Trust that He will lead you to
your Adam.
That you will be found by him.

The world goes
round,
round,
and round
again.
Everyone is moving
and everyone is *searching*.
Yet, I am trying to stay still
to hear my Maker's voice.
I, too, am searching
in quiet desperation.
I am in need of something
but don't know what.
I thought I would never end up here,
wherever here actually is.
But I am here.
Searching.
And listening.
While the world is still going round.
While the people are constantly moving and searching.
Yet I,
remain still.
I don't want to miss Him.

Some days...
all I feel like I
have to offer
is a cute face and
a nice shape...

Oh...
and this radiant
smile of mine.
I force myself
to work with
what I have,
the external.

Yet...
my internal
is caving in,
shattering into
pieces.

"Who am I?"
I look in the
mirror
and my mind
seems to draw a
blank,

emptiness is what
I feel,
a very close
friend indeed.

Suffering from
heartaches
pained so deeply
from a life of
misfortune,

Chaos...
and unending
heartbreaks.
A sense of
unworthiness
and rejection
floods my mind.

A burning stake
driven through
my heart.
Darkness
veils my eyes
and pushes me
back

into yet another
corner.
I'm cornered.

*"How could I ever
be what He wants
of me?"*
are the questions
that haunt me
continuously.

Day after day...
bits of pieces
of what I saw as
my identity
are drifting away.
I'm drifting
away...
in this abyss of
time.

"Who am I?"
are the thoughts
echoing through
my mind.
No one knows,
sees,

nor understands
my war.
No one knows,
sees,
nor understands
how torn I am.

I have been
machete-ed
immensely
and left open
wide.
Tears filling my
eyes
while the pain
goes deeper,
and deeper,
leaving me
wailing on the
inside.

"Please...
No more!"
as I cried and
begged.

"Please...
No more!"
are all the words I
said.

My house I live in is made out of
glass.
Fragile yet see through,
but was not designed to last.
The pieces keep falling
one **glass** at a time.
Trespassers come and go
and leave me more broken than blind

One blow to my mind.
One blow to my heart.
Another to my spirit,
and I'm left completely in the dark.
Cracked.
Desolated.
And naked for the world to see.
I'm daily being robbed
from my hope, joy, and securities.
My tenants are filthy,
unyielding, and relentless.
I'm occupied with vile strangers
who are driving me senseless.

Strength and courage,
who were once housed within me to nourish,
have been evicted by despair and pain,
and among others
who I care not to name.
I'm abandoned.
I'm void.
So why not bulldoze me?
I'm already destroyed!

…Wait.
What's that I hear?
A knocking at the door?
A knocking on my heart?
A piercing light infiltrating my darkness?
This voice that I hear says
"Let me in"
with a gentle tone.
But so ashamed of my filthiness
I rather be left alone.

Yet to my surprise,
He was persistent and quite a gentleman
and I can tell from His integrity
that He wanted to move in.
He wanted to rebuild me
and came with great authority
and immediately demanded the others to
"Move out!"
He says to me,
*"I am making you over
and it won't be this*
glasshouse.*"*

How could you love me?
When I constantly do my dirt,
purposely committed to my
sins
because on the inside I am
hurting
from within.
How could You love me?
When I repeatedly spit on
Your name
with my profane horrid mouth
and my senselessly saying
Your name in vain.
How could you love me?
When I choose to choose to
do my wrong.
Living without a care in the
world,
without a conviction,
without any guilt,
I am living for me all the day
long.
How could You love me?
When I don't even love
myself.
I refuse to look in the mirror
without the thought or notion
of killing myself.
My father raped me
and my childhood escaped
me.
I am dirty and I am unworthy
and here I am without a care
and without a worry,
for the pain I feel
is too hard to bury.
I am disgusted.
I am ashamed.
I am nothing.
And it seems like my life will
never change.
So why do You love me?
Why do You even care?!
And then I heard a small voice
that said:

"**Because** *I was always there.*
Since the beginning of
time
I ordained you as
mine.
I called you forth
from out of your
mother's womb
and not a day later
or a second too soon.
I ordained you a
prophet.
I ordained you a
queen.
I ordained you a ruler.
A leader.
And in My heart
you mean everything
to Me.

*You are beautiful
and I made you
unusual.
And the trials that you
have faced,
you have overcome
them because
I have given you My
grace.
So run your race
Because you are
destined to win.*

*And this I know
because I know
Your beginning to your end.
I have given you a new life through
My Son Jesus Christ.
And I am filling you up
with a love and a wholeness
which you won't be able to contain.
An explosion in your spirit,
a bubbling forth out of your mouth,
to the world you will proclaim,
that the goodness of God
has erased your shame.
And from this moment on
You will never be the same,
because I, Your God,
have changed your name."*

Life had a way of breaking her down.

For so long she had been painting a canvas of a life that really wasn't hers. One canvas after another, black paint being thrown onto each and every painting.
*"Do over
Wait…let's start again…
But this time with new friends
And new sets of circumstances."*

She was an avid skilled incorporator, who has incorporated a diversity of things to mold and shape her very own being. Yet and still it was a false image, nonetheless, God's image of her.

Backed into a corner with nowhere to turn, her mind was racing and those temporary quick fixes were just that…quick fixes. Leaving her broken…

yet again.

No more black paint being thrown…

And no more do-overs.

She was tired of painting a life that was not her own.

The many pieces of her were left widely scattered.

Scrambled.

And too
numerous to
gather.

Yet alone to try
and put herself…
Of what she
thought back
together.   There was
                         nothing left in her
                          but a loud
She was too   voice….
   weak.   screaming…   *"LORD I*
  Helpless.   *SURRENDER!"*
  Confused.
  And empty.

On this day
I give myself away.
On this day
I choose to do it Your way.
Life has shown me that
I can't do this on my own.
The more I try,
the more I fail,
the more I continue to do my wrong.
I want and desire what is right.
I want and desire **Your will** for my life.
So if that comes to denying myself
in order to put You first,
then I will die
so I may then live
to become what Jesus calls
the Church.

I looked for you,
the both of you,
only after I was completely
emptied of myself.
My selfishness.
The hurt.

And disgust.

I never took a second,
another thought,
to think
how might
my choices
have had affected you.

And now...
I'm sorry.
I'm truly sorry for giving you
up.

For erasing
and robbing you
from your timelines of life.
Of explorations.
Of developments.
From your choices.
Your dedications with God.

So I look for you,

the both of you,
in the faces of children that
run, walk, laugh,
giggle, wiggle,
and cry
right pass me.

And I can only wonder...
"would Centra have done it over?"
Would she have taken the
time
if given the chance
to be your mother?

Who would you have been
if I didn't commit not one
but two
acts of **sin**?

The waters are raging in my heart
and my soul is tearing me apart.
Conflicted with toxic emotions.
Trying to move forward
but I'm drowning
in this deep black raging ocean.
Self-disdain.
Stricken by pain.
Unrestrained feelings.
Lord I need your healing
because these waters
are raging.
Dictating and overtaking the love you
gave me.
Please save me...
from myself,
from the hurt I experienced from
everyone else.
Please save me...
because I keep suppressing
and I keep repressing
yet all the while
I keep digressing.
Please save me...
because I'm bound
by fears and confusion,
so many unspoken years,
and the tears are spilling over.
I'm at the end of my rope,
desperately holding onto
my one last hope.
Please save me....
and so I begin to pray...
let the peace of God flow

into my raging heart today.
Lord quiet the waters.
Stillness.
Because this moment on
I choose **forgiveness.**

It has been a constant struggle.
Us.
But I know it has to be this way.
Us separated.
Yet, I can't stop thinking about you
even when I know deep down
in my heart
this is what I had to do.
I had no choice or no room for decision.
I was force to let you go
to free myself
in order to be myself.
By myself.
Not with you,
only with God,
and no one else.

Our supreme ruler, omniscient God,
holds the master plan in His hands.
Because He knows and He understands
that we have to grow in Him
in order to grow from within.
And when He is finished
We will be able to transcend
and reach new heights
and break down barriers.

Because real love is His love
and the closer we are to Him,
the closer we are together.
The sky is the limit but the cost of it
is denying ourselves
and to remain committed.
Traveling down this narrow gate
and abased valley
alone.
Willing to be stripped naked,
pressed and pulled,
molded and shaped,
to be conformed to the man and woman
that God has predestined and ordained.

Indeed, it is a process and we are going through the refiner's pit.
No, it won't feel pretty
but we can't be so quick to quit.
Although it is a scary thing to be
separated
from the one you truly love.
But I have to ignore all fleshly emotions
and begin to start trusting
in the Man above.

So with the tears constantly flowing
and my heart skipping every other beat.
My stomach is turning
and I'm starting to feel weak.
The thoughts are weighing heavy
and my mind is racing
but I have to keep chasing
and stop contemplating and run after Him.
No matter what it appears like,
I have to keep my heart on guard,
and truly discern that Satan is a fraud.
And also a liar.
The father of all lies,
and I refuse to live my life in defeat.
I can't give up because enough is enough!
There is a much greater work taking place within the both of Us.
And we have to grow up!
So where do we go from here, despite our doubts and our fears?
I say take it one day at a time.
Whether if it's in sunshine or rain,
we must come to a realization and acceptance
that we are in a season
of **growing pains.**

I am breaking free
from impossibilities.
I am breaking free
from the fear and the guilt that you have
tormented me with.
I am loosening my grip from off this deadly friendship.
This relationship is toxic like asbestos and no longer will
I inhale you in.
No longer will you keep me in sin.
No longer.
Satan.
Will you win.
Therefore, I'm cutting all ties
And I'm breaking free from all your prison of lies.
Each day I'm growing in truth,
realizing more and more that I was a vessel that you chose to use,
chose to misuse, abuse, and confuse.
I was your dangling puppet.
Your instrument.
Your chick on the side.
But I've learned that there were others…
Yes, there were others…
that you've also taking on for the ride.
The ride to hell which is
harmless and fun
so, it's easy to sell.
It's easy to promote deception while deceiving the majority,
so that you in return may increase in authority!
It's easy to disguise and malnourish yet encourage the minds
to react off of every fleshly impulse,
which leads to sinful decisions,
but ultimately and strategically
you create division!

It's easy to blind the eyes and create a delusional world
that pride their eyes on
sex,
money,
and power.
All lies!
You are such a coward
and a cheat!
You don't care about me or the rest of this world,
all you care to broadcast the message of retreat.
"Retreat,
Retreat,
t*o your sinful nature!"*
Instead of the message of reconciliation to God.
Our Lord.
Our Maker.
And our Savior
So...
So long to all those wrongs.
So long to that girl you've
oppressed,
depressed,
and repressed.
So long to all that mess!
Because you've just lost that one.
Because this one,
chose to choose to walk with the Son.
And it's not over
because this battle has just begun between me and you.
And because of him
I am free
and I now have the victory over you!
Yes, Satan, I'm calling you out!
I'm exposing you!

I'm announcing to the world that you are a liar!
And I'm growing more and more wiser
and all the *lies* that you've told me were
just...
Lies.
So...
I'm turning my back on you.
I've had enough of you.
It's over...
Goodbye.

Your love is the theme of a song that **I never knew**.
So what is this virtue that I now carry?
Words hidden so deep.
Buried.
Speaking to me
in whispers
of great mysteries,
concerning Your divinity,
Your supreme power.
And I've gotten lost
in hours of time
just passing me by
of wondering,
thinking over and over...
"Why?
Why Lord did you choose me?"
Who am I that you are so mindful of me?
You must be mistaken,
haven't You seen my past?
The addictions.
The cursing.
The rebellion.
I've given my last
to only receive
nothing
in return.
I have nothing
but scars and burns
and heartbreaks
that continues to ache
after a love that is...
real.
A love that can truly...
heal

...and fill
this emptiness
of mine.
Yet, Your Love,
Oh, Your Love,
is a theme
of a song
I never knew.
So I take what remains,
all of this pain,
and as my offering
I give it all to you.

Is it all in vain?
This way of living in this world,
Is it all in vain?
All of the clothes,
friends,
money,
and significant others
don't mean one thing.
They don't measure to the joy
and hope You bring.
God You make my heart sing.
I am at peace with You.
I can't find true happiness
in these temporal things.
I sit here empty
well…
restless
Well not even that….
I just feel…
…how do I feel?
I feel as though I don't need to chase
the things of this world.
I don't need the clothes.
The friends.
The money.
This world.
I need You, Lord.
I need You.
Nothing else compares to You.
My real life is hidden in You.
Every time I try to substitute a way
that doesn't include you to fill this void
I feel like this,
I feel like sh*t.

I need more of You
Lord excuse my French.
I can't fill my desires because this flesh
like scripture says,
is like a bottomless pit.
I need substance.
I need truth.
It's time out
for this frivolous way of living.
I want more.
I want.
I need.
I desire...
You.

In the depths of my heart
I love you.
There is no deeper thing
no greater thing
than Your love.
Your love, Your love, Your love,
That is all I need to get me
through
these times,
these days,
that keep pressing and
weighing in on me.
Your love is all I will ever need.
I will hold on to it
because I am made strong in
it.
God, wrap me in Your arms.
Protect me.
Cover me.
Shield me from the evils and
dangers
of this world.
From those wicked people
who try to
devise,
deceive
and destroy.
Mend my broken heart
back to its full capacity.

Make me whole.
Wash me clean.
Lord, I just need you to love
on me.
Because my life
will come to nothing without
Your grace.
Forever Your love takes me
away,
to that secret place,
where I lay prostrate on my
face.
In your presence, it is just me
and you,
You and me,
all the daylong like an
unending love song.
Your love, Your love, Your love,
how it whisks me away.
I am a little girl again
but born again.
Fearless.
Joyful.
And full of laughter.
Well that's what it feels like…
Complete freedom.
Because **Your Love**, Lord,
is what I am after.

The world is never silent.
The world is never still.
So we wait impatiently for things
to open themselves up and reveal.
Revealing the unexpected truths
of the choices we make.
Because He has already given us the liberty
to choose which pathways
either death or life to take.
Yes, Lupe,
The world is ours.
But it is **here today and gone tomorrow.**
That's what life is and that's what people
tend to forget.
See no one really quite understand
what the meaning of truth really is.
Because in the darkened heart of a man
truth is nowhere to be found.

But what are there,

are the lies and deceptions

of his life

that keeps him steadily bound.

So there is no movement.

And his heart...

He can't use it.

No matter how bad and hard

we kick and fight

to grab hold of the things we think matter

in this life,

they are impeding our process,

and most importantly

they are stunting our growth.

Just like water

streaming through our hands

down to the fingertips

because it's too slippery to grasp.

Look around you,

this thing we call life,

was not intended to last.

Here today and gone tomorrow.
That's the story of my life.
The day to day struggles
that brings me so much strife.
Here today and gone tomorrow.
That's the time we foolishly use.
Instead of using it on a people
and our purpose,
which is to love,
we use it on self-indulgence
and we begin to lose.
Here today and gone tomorrow.
That's what this never silent world
is screaming all around us.
Because even she knows
that this world will soon
one day
come to a close.

(Song: "Fire, I see, fire raining down towards me. Fire, I see, fire raining down towards me.)

Your love for me is like a **consuming fire**,
and it sweeps me away.
It trail-blazes through my hardships,
my hurts, and my pains,
and it takes me higher.
To a deeper place in You
that will fill my soul,
that will fill my every desire.
I'm lost in You.
I am perfected in You.
So no need for fear or worry
because I will never lose.
Not as long as I have You,
and not as long as I have Your grace.
Which keeps on keeping me day to day,
through the challenges,
which are indeed molehills,
that I continuously face.
Yet, You never forsake me Lord,
but You're forever
leading me the way to
Truth.
A *mysterious* wonder,
hidden deep in You.
I'm captivated by Your love.
I am awe-struck by Your great love for me.
It unveils my dark eyes and helps me see,
perfectly and clearly,
that I am more than what others think of me.
I am beyond what they may reason
or that they may see.

I am a glorious image,
this picture perfect masterpiece
of Your great love for me.
I am beautiful.
I am loved.
I am free.
I am your burning desire
Which indeed feels like a ***consuming fire***
raining down towards me.

(Song: Fire, I see, fire raining down towards me. Fire, I see, fire raining down towards me.)

Enjoy this moment.
For this could be your last.
Enjoy this moment.
For this too shall pass.
Life comes and life goes
and every single choice you make
is within your own control.
Every day is a mystery and who knows what the next day may bring.
The power in our lives comes
in how we choose to spend it.
The power in our lives show forth
in how we choose to live it.
Every person has a purpose
and only God knows
the correct way our lives should go.
He is the Author and Finisher
of our faith and our existence
and in Him only will we gain
our true image.
So enjoy this moment
because the promise of tomorrow
is not for certain,
and today could very well be your end.
Enjoy this moment.
Because this life we now see
is like a chasing after the wind.

You can have everything a man desires
but if you do not have God's love on the inside of you,
you have nothing.
You can be gifted,
talented, and skilled in many areas
but if you do not have love,
God's love,
then it is all meaningless.
You can possess all knowledge
from every field that you've gathered to and fro of the earth
but if you possess not His love,
you possess nothing.
You can gain all the riches,
wealth,
money,
and fame
but without God's love you gain nothing.
You can be the most popular,
most looked upon person,
you can represent what *man* calls a superstar,
but if you have not God's love on the inside of you,
I tell you what you are:
you are nothing.

I stress the significance of having the love of God in us
because without it we are nothing more
than a walking vapor taking up valuable space in the earth.
When you have God's love in you,
you put to good use all the acquired things you have:
all your possessions
and all your knowledge to bring forth
a positive difference and change.
You are not selfish but selfless.
You are not wreck-less but stable.

You paved the way for the next man,
for the next woman,
for the next child,
not even being mindful of color,
gender, or disability.

Because if God's love
is really operating on the inside of you,
He will reveal His purpose and plan for you.
You are the window of opportunity.
So you put yourself second and God's will first and
ask yourself: *"What God's love would have me do?"*
Then devote that same love He has freely given to you
and freely give it back to a particular pursuit or a people.

I've been keeping myself boxed in,
not knowing what's been keeping me in
this prison.
Locked up.
Thrown away the key
in this social media world
where I've grown too lax.
Too comfortable.
Merely looking outside
from the windows of these eyes
too deeply
into everyone else's thinking
except mine.
Who is she?
Is the question of the hour.
Yes, the subject of identity
that I refuse to see.
My own.
Yet, like a robot I am an enemy to me.
Forever scrolling
...liking...
 everyone else's lives
except self.
Indulging in everyone 's else's pics,
I need help.
Subconsciously using it as a standard
for my own measurement.
It doesn't make sense
how I use their lives as my
own comparison.
Now If beauty lies in the eyes of the beholder...
then why am I blind to it?
Why can't I admit
and commit

to really seeing
my uniqueness,
my own context
of beauty that is?
Ain't I worth beholding?
My story told and unfolding?
And should not my ideas, visions, dreams
thrive and be realized
outside?
Yea out there?
Instead of rather die
silently hidden
in here.
Within myself.
Within this skin that I am too afraid to stretch,
too afraid to dig beneath the surface,
dig right into the slits clefts and depths
of the dirt of where I now stand.
Wiggling my light brown toes in the sand.
Digging down in
the unearth.
The unspoken.
The unwritten.
The unsung.
The unheard.
Where I am seen flying in the deep blue sky.
Is that a plane?
Is that a bird?
It's locked up.
Thrown away the key.
Pandora's box is it?
Maybe not.
But I continue to question its validity.
What's so great about me?

Using my tongue as a weapon
to engage in the very act of my own self-deception.
"I'm not good enough...
I'm not smart enough.
This is wrong...
And that is wrong...
...When I speak my words
they Come out convoluted.
She does it better...
He rocks it better...
I'm too stupid."
It's locked up.
Thrown away the key.
My true self.
This prize that remains buried deep.
A bestowed jewel that God has given
to shake the earth from their own prisons.
An undiscovered life
that many will never know.
Untouched.
 Lost.
 Souls.
Because I chose not to grow.
It's locked up.
Thrown away the key.
By my hands,
I closed the door on
destiny.
Which will forever be a kept mystery
because I was too afraid of
setting
her
free.

I could've crumbled up
and died
because of how you made me feel
on the inside.
Who are you?
To tell me what's wrong is right
and what's right is wrong?
Unending accusations
never mending a broken song.
No, you are wrong.
And you have been all along.
And I was foolish and naïve to believe
the deceptions of truth that
lies beneath.
So I'm asking you nicely
to please take a seat.
And stop trying to knock me off my feet.
Pulling me under.
Tearing me open wide.
Asunder.
Like no other.
And for a second there,
I found myself bare,
naked, idle, confused,
and I knew you didn't care.

Yet, you didn't stop there.
It was just a continual cycle
of questioning whether if I
was worth the call
even after my many falls.
Even after every word
of slander and affliction
and all of the convictions of
my heart,
despite my addiction of pleasing
the ones who contradict Him.
I lost sight of my vision.
Which was to carry
on His mission.
The great commission
that is.
So I'm not going to let you run me
from my purpose.
No matter what you think my worth is because in Him
I am worth it.
I am worth the nails.
I am worth the cross.
I am worth the travail.
I was worth the tearing of the veil.
I know who I am.
I am in Christ and in Christ
I AM.

I am not your usual.
I would go as far as saying abnormal.
It took me a while realizing this
but I am unique.
Sweet.
Beautiful.
Loud.
And proud.
I
am
me.
Perfect and wonderfully made by my artist.
My Creator.
My whole reason of existence.
I was created in His likeness
and in His divine image.

Set apart from the world
but drawn close to my Lord.
Purposed and planned for a reason
for a specific season
and a specific time.
To a specific generation.
I'm just a specific kind.
I am flawed.
I am a mess.
Yet, I still stand tall.
Even when I do fall,
He picks me back up
because I am His all
and He is my all.

And His glory is the reason for my story.
I have been isolated.
Neglected.
Enslaved.
And rejected.

Humiliated.
Accused.
Criticized.
And even abused.

Just plain misunderstood
and left broken.
Nearly lost my mind.
Myself.
And to the point of just giving up…
just like that,
He raised me
from my lowest point
to the skies above.
He raised me.

Through His tender mercies,
unmerited favor
and His unquenchable multifaceted love.
He saved my life and changed my world.
He gathered my numerous broken,
shattered pieces,
and fashioned,
transformed
while yet still molding
and shaping me distinctly
into a beautiful mosaic art.
No I am not your usual.
I am not even perfect.
Maybe different.
Weird
or even abnormal.
But today I declare to you:
I am
unfinished.

Hey mama...**I'm sorry**.
And I know I have told you
this over and over again.
But I just didn't know...
I couldn't have known...
how you had rent
and spent
your life so violently
just to protect
your family.
And I'm sorry for blaming you.
And being *sooo* angry with you.
For not truly understanding
all that you had to go through
and what you had to suffer
just to be my mother.
And so I honor you today
with words
that are just too hard to express
without thankful tears
falling down to my chest...
I thank you mommy
for not giving up on me.
For believing me when I had told you
the truth,
even as a young girl
for me...
that was very hard to do.
And I praise you for being my superhero.
Although I didn't know at the time,
that you had been
in the business of saving your daughter
before the thought of me needing saving
had ever crossed my mind.

She is what words could not
paint
nor demonstrate
the essence of
self-less giving.
and I'm afraid...
that I won't say enough.
Using fragments of thoughts
to articulate
my sentiments of her...
barely.

That she is...
not just my mother...
but she is my other
half.
A blast from the past
worth recognizing,
worth honoring.
Not truly understanding
all that she fought through
just to carry and nurture
the seeds of her
womb.

<u>I have no clue.</u>

Nor did I understood her
fight,
and I'll probably never will.
And I could not travel
those same long distances,
walk those same long
miles in those very heels.

But I have finally become to
see
what God has blessed and
gifted, far from perfect, but
made perfectly for me...
The heart of a servant. The
soul of a warrior. I call her...
Queen.

I am tired of **hiding.**
Walking in the shadows
of those I confide in.
Because what I believe
that is in me,
is in no comparison
to the ones around me
that I see.
Yet, I begin to doubt,
And neglect His plan
for my plan
so...I'll figure it out!
I'll figure out how to win
the approval
and acceptance of others,
breaking tooth and nail
to try and get them to see me
for who I really am.
That I'm no longer
the girl they knew before.
That I'm no longer
that old feeble woe-man.
But it doesn't matter how
hard I fight and prove,
because fighting in the
flesh man is
where I begin to lose.
So this is where I choose
today
either to live for Him
or live for You.
And Lord I just want to
live for You.
Forget everyone else's
thoughts of me.
You are my choice, my voice,
You are simply the reason
why I see.
And in You I have
my true being,
but in them I have
no freedom.
Freedom to be the woman
You predestined me to be.
The unearthed part of me.
Which is Victorious.
Anomalous.
Earth-shaking.
Free.

I'm **flying**.
I'm flying up, up, up.
I'm flying going up.
Moving through storms so terrible,
yet I'm breaking through.
Where the sun shines.
Where Your heart meets mine.
No more burdens will I shoulder.
Not anymore.
Because I have given them over
into Your hands.
And freed the weight from off my feet
and I'm rising again.
Going up, up, up.
Chasing the sweet melodies…
Going up, up, up.
Those warm filling love notes…
Going up, up, up.

Hey black girl.
If I could trace the thread of your heritage
What would I find?
A million lost souls.
A million lost minds.
Blind to the truth
of their very existence.
Which have been intercepted
and oppressed
by misinformed
man-made decisions.
Concerning their identity,
stripped and robbed from their destiny
that has been orchestrated in the constellations above.
Salvation.
Inscribed by His undying love.
Hey black girl.
Did you know that your roots grow deep?
Deeper than the full texture of those kinks,
zigzag links and curly twists of your
tightly wound up hair that you wear?
Don't hide it any longer,
let the people stare!
Because those golden locks of pride
were meant to grace the sunlit sky
and roam free.
Defying the very essence of gravity
and depravity of the burning heat
and whips, and the untamed heat and whips
of the wind.
Did you know your skin,
in all its hues,
rays of colors
and warm shades,
is just as decorative from
the unfading beauty that
rests and glows from within?
Your skin

is beautiful.
Distinct yet beautiful.
You are a pure original
even if you don't see it.
Believe it.
Because the time is now
to undo the lies that have framed you,
shamed you and encaged you like
an unwanted black bird.
Whose voice has been silenced and whose song
unheard.
Hey black girl.
For centuries you were a kept mystery,
lost files scattered through a mixture of imageries
that were not you.
Lies embedded...more lies that they said were copacetic
but today... I give to you
what is rightfully yours...
The truth.

Confidence.
Is trusting...
And believing.
You are assured...
Beyond the shadow of doubt
Of this knowledge...
Of this understanding...
Of truth.

I have learned over the years
that hair does not define you.
It does not give you
a true since of value or worth.
It is what's inside of you.
That beautiful mind that God has given us.
The heart that makes
a person so conspicuous.
That alone is the drawing of true beauty.
It is not the superficial layer of a person
because as the years go by
that beauty,
that superficially catches the eye,
soon withers up and die.
Beauty is not skin deep.
Beauty is *unique.*

So what if your hair is red
blue, orange, green, or pink;
Nappy, curly, straight, kinky, or wavy.
God is the Creator of it all
and what I have is what He gave me.
I don't care if you are purple,
yellow, black or white.
You are His adoration and all that He made
He made it perfect and He made it right.
So go right on and express, change,
or just be plain Jane!
Be an individual.
Be you.
Be Beautiful.

I'm bursting through the ground.
Rooted down so deeply,
I feel myself stretching and growing,
breaking free from these dark
cramped spaces.
    I'm opening up in colors unimaginable.
     Beauty beyond eyes that are able
      to recognize and see me for
       who I really am.
He has arrayed me in the finest clothes:
Pedals of sunshine yellow, hello fuchsia,
fearless red, baby blue and white
so pure it's soul-cleansing!
     I'm washed by the light of His love,
      Which shines down from
       those sheer clear skies,
      leaving me mesmerized
      of a feeling so consuming,
     so breathtaking, as I bend
     and rock ever so gently
    by the wind of **His Presence.**

Live without ceasing,
in every moment that you are breathing,
God has given you breath for a reason.
So go ahead and purposely
live in every season.
Sometimes the test and trials of life
keeps us from living, but rather surviving.
Not even realizing that the Father
gave us His Son by dying,
so that we may be *revived* in Him.

Smoked, clogged factories.
Hot, sweaty, blood-bruised
hands.
Monotonous events
facing the daily demands.
Slave to a system.
Working for a dime.
Slave to a system.
Just to pass the time.
Punch in.
Punch out.
The same rhythmic pattern
around the clock.
Day shift.
Night shift.
The work just doesn't stop.

Those hands were made
to create
Beauty.
Yet what I see,
is a picture of poverty;
of impoverished mindsets.
Identities.
So subtly
being reduced
to machines.
Of men
who lost their hope
and never realized
their dreams.

Imprisoned by fears.
So many lost years.
From toil.

Toil.
Sweat.
And even more
toil.
Oppressed by the oppressor.
Slave to the master.
You build the economy!
You made him rich
faster!

And they watched you suffer.
They taunted you!
Exploited you!
Used you!
Abused you!
To build their empire.
Sacrificing your will.
Conforming your minds
to their desires!

Being made out of a fool.
Reduced to a mule.
A modern
day
machine
that is,
as a means to their
selfish ends
with your hot, sweaty,
blood-bruised hands.
Only to get in return,
a couple of pennies.
Only to get in return,
Nothing.

Why do we care
to dissect the thoughts
of mere men?
Their observations of life
defined by our shared human
skin?
That we addictively find
ourselves
wrapped in?
Why are their theories
So enticing?
So interesting?
No seriously.
Please enlighten me.
Help me help me you
understand my predicament.

Because the last time I check
we are no different
than the aimless blowing
of the wind.
We are no different
than the falling of
the leaves
that temporarily clothe
trees.
In and out of seasons,
the recycling of human beings.

So why are we so caught up
and amused
by man's
finite reasoning?

Casanova,
please cast me over
into the arms
of Your sweet love
again.

Let me ...
drown
face deep
into the depths
of the many grains
of good thoughts
that are referred by David
 as sand.

For I want to be lost
in the rhythms of
Your great complexities,
those secret mysteries
that goes fully
beyond
my vivid imagination.

See...
there is no equation
to figuring You out.
But I'll chase right after You
and that's without a doubt

I'll leap out of bounds,
skyrocket to the moons,
just to be in the grasps,
the very sight...
 of You.

Reset me.
And make me over.
For I want to be fully love by
You
Mr. ...
Casanova

The great American people.
The great European people.
From Japan to Iran
to African, Mexican,
and Indian people.
We are all people!
So why don't we treat one
another as equal?
Not according to color or
gender
or culture or language.
But by Gods love is where we
should aim it.
Where we should proclaim the
Name
Who was slain and through his
blood
and love for us we all are one
in the same.
All under one name.
All destined to win.
And break free
and loose ourselves
from the powers
and terrors of sin.
And if we continue so therein,
it will bring us to our end.
To our perdition because
God's plan is for remission.
Gods plan is for unity.
To unify all human beings and
that includes you and me.
He wants to illuminate our
eyes so that we may see.

See past the pain.
See past the temporal worldly
gains like fame...
and **see**.
See pass seeing,
Which is sooo freeing!
See the freedom which awaits
for us in His kingdom!
See the love that is showered
unto us daily from the Man
above!
See truth.
See me.
See you, him, and her.
We all are a part of and
destined
for His everlasting virtue.
It goes beyond this earthly
temple.
Who knew?
It goes beyond
the color distinctions
and how we are particularly
framed.
It goes beyond
what meets the eye.
It's a life change experience.
And I'm talking to you and to
every person in the world
to incline their ear
in hearing it.
Truth is ...
We are all called to be
brothers and sisters,

united together, made in His image and His likeness. Created and I mean specifically designed to live forever.

Are
You
Awake?
Do you hear?
Do you see?
Life?
Taste.
Smell.
See.
Touch.
Warm skin,
blood flowing like a river
in every facet of your being.
Red.
Blue.
Can I comfort you
through words to
awaken you to
life?
Clouds high in the sky.
Green grass sweeping the earth.
Dirt.
Do you know your worth?
Rays of light dawning from the sun,
illuminating this realm,
His Glory.
Nature is telling a story.
Painting a clear picture.
She's speaking.
Day unto day
uttering forth speech.
Night unto night
revealing knowledge.
Sunrise.
Sunset.
Spring.
Summer.
Winter.
Fall.
Just telling it all.
Are you listening?
She's narrating a narration
in you
all around you...
Creation.
Mocking birds singing
a song,
praising.
Squirrels climbing trees,
playing.
Wind gently whistling,
blowing.
Cool, crisp, clean air,
invisible
yet blowing.
Touch.
Do you feel it?
Can you hear the song?
That they all sing along?
Praising.
Glorying.
Living.
Life.
Are
you
awake?

These black, brown, white,
yellow, and orange bodies
that we **confine** ourselves to,
that we pride ourselves to,
limits and narrows
our spiritual vision.
Where we are left blinded
and deafened to
understanding
that in *real* reality
we were purposely
predestined
to be remade
in Christ's image.
Yes, black is beautiful,
and so are the other various
shades
of the spectrum, too.
Yet *who we really are*
is much fairer than skin color.
But I guess the truth
is really indeed offensive.
Too expensive to buy.
So we rather depreciate
our value
at the cheap cost
of believing a lie.

There's no one who can think like me.
There's no one who can talk like me.
There's no one who can feel the things that I feel
because **I am an original**.
There's no one who can see like me.
There's no one who can dream like me.
There's no one who can be the best me that I am
because I am an original.
I am no carbon copy.
And I won't be defined by nobody.
Not by society.
Not by my environment.
Not by the family and friends who I grew up with.
Not by my hurts and not by my pain.
I won't let it rule me no longer
and I will not allow it to be my shame.
Because I now where a new name.
And His name is Christ.
My righteousness.
My redeemer.
My life.
And I,
Oh, and I,
will sing His Name to the highest heights
and I will speak His truth and His wisdom to the lowest lows.
There is no foe
except the one that is found right beneath your nose.
You are what you speak.
You are how you think.
You are a product of what you believe.
You are in control of your destiny.
You are gifted and are filled with vision,
creativity, and longevity.

So tap in it.
Because...
There's no one who can think like you.
There's no one who can talk like you.
There's no one who can feel the things that you feel,
because you are an original.
There's no one who can see like you.
There's no one who can dream like you.
There's no one who can be the best you that you are
because you are an original.
There's no one who can look like you
or dress the way you do
or be the best at you are
because my brother and my sister,
you are an original.
You are.
You are.
And I am
God's handmade original.

Life is so much more than what we see.
It's not about the temporal things,
but our eternal being.
We get so caught up
in the things we glory in,
like celebrities, and their lives,
and the cars they drive in.
But let me ask you this one thing,
when will **our story** ever begin?
When will we transcend
and break down walls
and emerge forth
into the life that we were all called?
And that's aligning ourselves with God.
Our story, is not about all the things
and possessions we acquired,
or all the lustful and fruitless stuff
we desired.
Our story starts through all the souls
and lives we inspire.
So let's go higher.
When will we stand bold
and declare to the world,
"Enough is enough?!"
When will we stop being pulled
by every wind of doctrine
to every direction that is presented in front of us?
Life or shall I say this *Christian life,* that is,
is about diverging from the norm.
It's about being set apart.
Just because everybody is following
some course of action and conforming
to a social standard, doesn't make it right!
Just because the world says "yes"
we say "yes" too!
I would have to question the validity
of such a movement when I know
in the back of my mind

and in my heart, that it has to be
much more to it.
I'm just saying.

Song: "Dream dreamer.... you're a dreamer. Dream dreamer...you're a dreamer.")

I call you...Joseph.
Joseph.
Look up and tell me the vision that you see?
I give it to you,
your destiny.

Don't you see
how the stars line up
like the big dipper?
And so I dip down in
the basin of My galaxies
and pour you out a cup,
like a river,
running over,
of My many blessings.

No.
This isn't a fantasy.
More like mental *clarity*
of what I had already set up for you
from the beginning.
Before time
wound herself back
and started tic-*king*.
Don't you know I called you to
reign and rule
as **King**?
Don't you know
Queen
who I created you to be?

I call you Joseph.
Joseph.
Don't you see your dreams?
All of the promises that I had secretly
tucked into your mind
while you were sleeping
through time.
The many treasures that I have
enclosed in your heart.
Hidden.
Waiting to be risen
up out of you.

See, it was in the dark
where I shed My light
into your night
whispering your fears away.
And I gave to you revelations
concerning the coming manifestations
of the fruitful years
where you would walk this earth
in My ways.
And I will use you mightily
Joseph
in these last and evil days.

I've called you
to be just like me:
an extraordinaire
supernatural
Genius
with intellectual power.

And you shall build
with your hands
strong towers.
While the nations will
run to you
and dance
in the wind.
And your song
will bring healing
to the weary, broken soul.
And the words that
I will speak through you
will draw my lost sheep
back unto the fold.

Don't you know who you are?
Jossseeeeph.
Joseph.
Joseph!

Eyes wide open,
but are you awake
to your dreams?

Blank spaces,

my life was once filled with

blank spaces.

Just a mumbo jumbo of unruly

characters

disjointed,

randomly juxtaposed together.

No sequence of time,

I was going out of my mind

with these blank white spaces.

That held me in a very

limbo state of…

My voice was
made
to soothe ears
and dry tears
of the broken-
hearted...

                My voice was
                made
                to soothe ears
                and dry tears
                of the broken-
                hearted...

                                My voice was
                                made
                                to soothe ears
                                and dry tears
                                of the broken-
                                hearted.

Yesterday...
it was as if I was another
person.
The things I use to say
like...
There's no me without you.
Or how I worshiped
the ground you traveled
with your size 13 feet shoes.

You were my focus.
I saw you as God.
Tall as the amazon,
my heart couldn't fathom
just how awesome you were.

The one who would forever
shelter me.
Protect me.
Love me.
And tell me that I was
beautiful.

But today...
now that you are gone...
I was forced to grow up.
To finally learn
and see...
that I was enough.

And yea...
it hurt,
like hell it did.
It hurt like
sh*t.

But as time passed by
I had to get over it,
and reckon with the truth,
with the real question:
*"Who am I
without you?"*

Who is this woman that
God saw fit to use?

To think of
before her body parts came
together
in her mother's womb?

When she was just an
intentional
thought in His great galaxy of
a mind.
Is she awesome?
...I was curious to know
her real design.

And although delirious
from the wounds that I have
suffered.
I took my feeble legs
(my size 8 feet shoes)
and traveled
in worship.

I had to discover her
for myself.
As bad as it was hard to
breathe,
I was desperate and hungry
to know...
my identity.

I'm starving my fears
and I'm strengthening my faith.
Too much to do to stay stagnant,
oh no, not in this place.
So I have to chase… after Him,
or my light, which is His life in me, will eventually grow dim.
Now what benefit is that for you or me?
Especially when He pulled me out of darkness,
so the whole world could see,
so the whole world could be free.
I'm starving my fears
and I'm strengthening my faith.
No longer will I doubt or wonder.
No longer will I contemplate
whether I can trust my Father.
Whether I can trust my faith, which is really His faith
in Him.
These old dry bones could do nothing
without His spirit, His life,
Christ.

And all these visions, dreams, and promises
are His desires,
which He freely gave to me,
so I could rise
higher.
Yet, the contradictions, that the devil
relentlessly throws at me,
surrounds me with,
blinds my eyes totally…
where I'm consumed in my emotions.
Drowning in the fears, cares, and worries of this unbelief ocean.
This cataclysmic explosion
of polar opposites.
Opposing what my Father said is and will soon be.
The devil keeps playing with my mind where it's preventing me to
see.
I'm fighting this fight of faith.

Clinching to my Father's unchanging hand
continually day after day.
But if I can be honest with myself,
and truly honest with myself.
And pull off the veil of my secrecy
to find lying there underneath,
holding me captive
is my *unbelief*.

Yes, it's my unbelief that is holding my faith ransom!
Trying to stricken it down and eat away at it like a cancer!
No more will I allow you to block and hold me down!
No longer will I be silenced with the cares of this world
Bound!
Paralyzed by fears.
Crying over and over again with so many tears,
over these irrational stupid fears!
Like…dude…
you're not even real!
But used by the enemy to steal destroy and kill
my faith!
No devil you made a huge mistake!
With your cunning, tired -down, worn-out trickery.
I've been awakened and never forsaken
by truth
and now
I see!
And now I choose to believe.
So I'm dismantling this unbelief.
Breaking it down with the word of God and
crushing it under my feet,
so I can rise
higher.
In His love.
Soaring with wings stretched out like an eagle
in the blue skies above.
Out of this grim dark pit,

won't have me circling around
nobody's wilderness!
So I'm taking no thought
and I'm playing a new sound,
playing my trumpet up in the air
with my feet planted fixed on the ground.
Declaring to the world aloud and proud:
**I'm starving my fears
and I'm strengthening my faith.**
"Because it's a new season…,"
says the Lord,
"And it's a new day."

I could have told you,
how I still loved you,
even at the tender age of
eight.
After you had raped the
dreams
and serenity
right from out of me
but...
you left.
Yet...
I still loved you anyway.

Remarkably,
Purity in my eyes still
looked at you as
my father,
my daddy
...my papa.
And I longed for you
to return back home.

I really don't know the
specifics
or what had truly gone wrong
with you in your childhood
to cause you to sing
such a dark song.
To cause you to falter,
to slaughter, and strip away
the many innocence
of your sons and daughters.
Yet...
I decided long ago

to forgive you anyway.

Despite the abuse.
Despite how I had to journey
on the many years without
you.
Misused.
Falling subject to the hands of
endless men who repeated my
trauma
(but this time with me
willingly)
all over again.

Or the many times I cried to
myself
after watching my friends with
their parents.
Seeing their happiness.
That protection
...the hugs that they felt...
I hated that you left
and left me broken
and unspoken for...
yet **I chose to love you
anywa**y.

And I chose to move on,
in hopes,
and with fragile notes
to sing a new song.
Praying diligently,
that your absence

would not be the end of me.

But a girl could only hope...
Yea...
this now woman still desires
to hope for and help
you
revisit the horrors of yours
and our
past,
and fix what became horribly
bad.
Because more than you will
ever know,
I still want to love you
anyway...**Dad**.

Patience.
That word sometimes
gives me the *cringe*.
Because at times
I just want to live.

No restraints.
Without consequences.
Owning my moments
of the choices I make,
even if they are the wrong
ones.

Yet...
from my own experiences
I have sorely learned,
oh how life can burn.
Singe
the very flesh
right off your body.
Because I was so quick,
too quick,
to be...
quick.

Patience,
is love
suffering long,
for people
who you really
(*don't*)
care for.

It is denying
your will
to purchasing things you
know you can't afford.

Patience,
is humbling.
It is more being still
and less grumbling.

It is an admittance of
*"hey...I really don't have all
the answers."*
And that I'm okay
with waiting,
even after waiting.

It is a mindset.
A trust.
An understanding
that you are not just
doing life by yourself,
but there is Someone
always by your side
whispering,
*"never
give
up."*

The cries of my heart emptied out on paper.
Wet ink and dry erasers.
And so I share what is hidden,
secretly buried.
My love for you is so strong.
Only if you knew
the weight of my heart,
the weight of my love,
the weight of my song.
Only if you knew
the wait of my heart,
the wait of my love,
the wait of my song.
Only if you could feel
the red rivers and currents
of red water that pushes against
the encaged.
The ripples of beating.
My deepest cares
stripped bare
in open view.
Seething, like a tunnel
of wind
cycling at speeds
too fast for you to perceive
my love for you.

I want to be held
how a baby is held
in the arms of her mother.
Cradled.
Protected by the unseen dangers
that her gaze can measure.
I want to be told
that beauty is the sight of you.
It is the sound that your voice utters.
It is the thoughts
that cannot be tangibly grasped.
Unless one could ask,
"Exactly... what are you thinking?"
And I'll just let out a faint laugh,
because the complexity yet simplicity
of that question can go unanswered.
But I'll let you muse on me
because I want to be
a kept mystery
by you.
I want you to unveil and unfold
every layer of meaning.
And **I want you to see** me
for who I really am.
I want you to see into me
and feel the unrecognizable.
And dig deep
down into my soul.
And unearth the real treasures
of my heart.
Because
I am much more
than
body
parts.

(Song: *Here's what I like about you. That's what I like about you. You're open...you're open.*)

I'm
so
open.
Caught up,
wide open,
to share
the unspoken.
And I
won't
hold back
anymore.
Because...
You did not hold back
Your love for me!
You did not hold back
Your suffering,
Your
Self-sacrificing,
Self-serving
love
on Calvary.

No.
You let yourself bleed
out:
red
drops
of living
warm
flowing
blood,

did you bleed
for me.

And you,
hung there.
And you,
hung there.
And you,
hung there.
Stripped
bare.
Because that's how much
You cared
for my life
to
be
spared.

So I...
made up in my mind,
I ...
made up in my mind
this time,
that every heartache,
pain,
that I've
endured,
that I've
experienced,
was not a mistake.

Every tear that I have shed
when I thought
I would limp over

dead,
was for
a purpose.

To birth within me,
a
new way of breathing,
a
new way of seeing,
thinking,
living,
life.

I'm listening hard.
   Can't stop
   penciling
   the thoughts
   You speak
   concerning me.

As I **wait** for You,
   like how
   the watchman
   wait for the
   morning,
I wait for You.

I will be
Your watch-
woman.
Still.
Ears open to hear
Your
Word.

I will go where
You
send me to go,
and I will speak
boldly,
but in love,
what You tell me
to speak.

For You Lord are
my destiny,
and that is finally
clear to me.
You are my being.
You are my Truth.

And I will
continue on
as I sing this song
desiring
to please
You.

This song in my heart
that I'm unable to articulate.
A song worth penciling,
yet it's hidden deep inside of me
pumping harder than I can breathe.
This resounding rhythm
too inexpressible for meaning.

It's locked up.
Yet, I'm caught up,
desiring to set her free.
"Catch the little foxes"
You say

"Be patient. And don't allow them

to spoil your vine. Don't mix old with the new grapes of flowing wine.

You are beautiful,
a rose worth giving,

strikingly unusual,

a masterpiece worth finishing.

Daughter don't awaken love before it's time...

"Patience"

You say.

...And so
I listen.

100

Captivated by every step
that I take with You,
I walk with You,
hidden.
Forgiven.
Closed eyes wide-open to Truth.
I exhale and I breathe
believing for the first time
in my life
of really seeing You
for who You really are.
A painted picture of love
far beyond my deepest creative imaginations.
And so *I let it all go*.
I cast to you
all my songs of woes,
and I dance
in Your rain that cleanses
and washes away the pain
from my past.

I am fearfully,
wonderfully,
and beautifully made.
I am a work of art,
a beautiful display of an illustration
and clear description of a woman...
God has made.
Woven together with intricate
creative,
yet thoughtful care.
I am God's child
who dare can compare.

He thought me up before the world ever existed.
There was no doubt in His mind.
No inkling of uncertainty in His vision.
No random accident.
No deep drawn out explanation.
I Am that *I Am*.
No conflict of hesitation.

There was no mistake when He created me
because His purpose and His plan
was to tailor **a Queen**.

I am triune being,
spirit,
soul,
and
body.
And in His very eyes
I am somebody.

I am Christ's body.

I am His love.
And the reason why His Love...
died for His love.
I am the full walking representation
of what a woman of God should be.

I am the living Word.
I am a gift to this earth.
Packaged,
wrapped,
and made perfectly complete.
So, no matter what you say,
and no matter what you think,
 I am His Story.
 I am His Glory.

(Song: Victorious, Victorious, I am Victorious
…. Victorious.)

Victory.
God's sweet gift to me.
He has seated me on high
my El Shaddai says:
"Follow Me closely and you shall never die."
I am exalted by my King and for this reason I sing:

"Victorious, Victorious, I am Victorious
…. Victorious"

I have loosed myself from every fear.
Watered my crops with so many tears.
Broke away from this decaying pain
towards my life
my Lord,
my gain.
"Walk with me and I'll show you the way
This I know because I told you to say:

"You are Victorious, Victorious, you are Victorious
…Victorious."

He has changed my world ever since I was a girl.
Gave me new life
which is hidden in Christ.
Opened new doors and left me floored.
Brought me into His palace
and transformed my being.
Dressed me with His royalty
and now I stand as His Queen singing:

*"I am Victorious, Victorious, I am Victorious
…. Victorious."*

Some things...
can't be explained...
by...
human knowledge.

They are
because they are
just like God is
because...
He
just
is.

Just like I am
who I am,
and Whose I am
rest and abides
within me.

I am **supernatural**
filled with a power
that is eternal
so it makes me unnatural.

And my uniqueness,
my uniqueness is what defines
me as...
unfamiliar.

So they ask...

"Who is she?"
That's what they all ask
and that's what they all
wonder.
Which cause their minds
to ponder
because their blind eyes
can't see.

Because if they really
knew me,
without finite reasoning
they wouldn't question my
being.

I am a peculiar creature
with distinct features,
which features
a past of disgrace and shame
to a present of me now
knowing His Name,
to a future of praise to the
God who saves.
My walk is destined.
And my steps are indeed
ordered.
And the people I encounter...
I
call
blessed.

If I could paint my life
like I would a picture...
I wouldn't just draw straight lines
and doodling images.
No, I would paint **blue skies**
and brilliant colors.
Yes, *blue skies* and brilliant colors.

When poetry
is not enough.
When my heart and soul
is tired of writing
this stuff.
I'll *run* to You.

Just like how a child runs
to the arms of her father
I'll run... to You...
Lord.

www.ingramcontent.com/pod-product-compliance
Lightning Source LLC
Chambersburg PA
CBHW050915160426
43194CB00011B/2414